Anchored in Kindness

A Fruit of the Spirit Devotional for Kids

JENNA MAYE THOMPSON

Contents

1 What Is Kindness?

"[22] But the fruit of the Spirit is love, joy, peace, forbearance, kindness, goodness, faithfulness,[23] gentleness and self-control. Against such things there is no law."
Galatians 5:22-23

Have you ever heard of the Fruit of the Spirit before? It's a term in the Bible that references nine (9) different qualities that a person who knows and loves God can receive from the Holy Spirit.

Are you picturing apples and bananas right now?
Me, too!

However, what this verse is referring to is that the *fruit* is the result of hard work.

When you work really hard on a drawing or a very special project, and it turns out great, you get to enjoy the "***fruit of your labor***" and display it so that everyone can see it.

Do you understand what the word "fruit" in this verse means now?
It is so meaningful!

When we let the Holy Spirit work in our lives, we get to receive love, joy, peace, patience, kindness, goodness, faithfulness, gentleness, and self-control.

Those are the nine (9) fruits of the Spirit. We are going to be studying kindness and how to apply it to our lives to see a bountiful "harvest"!

Are you ready?

~Time To Pray~

Lord, please help me to be kind today, even if someone is unkind to me. Open my heart and mind to be able to see opportunities to love people by showing them kindness. I know that it won't always be easy, but I am going to try my best. With your help, I know I will succeed!
Amen.

KINDNESS CONVERSATIONS

What is your **favorite fruit?**

What are the **9 Fruits of the Spirit?**

Why do you think **kindness** is so important?

"[12] Therefore, as God's chosen people, holy and dearly loved, clothe yourselves with compassion, kindness, humility, gentleness and patience."
Colossians 3:12

Do you know how to be kind?
Here's a little tip.

Kindness starts with caring, being tender-hearted, and compassionate towards others. Jesus shows us how to love and be kind in the Bible.

Did you know that He actually washed his friends' feet?
Would you wash your friends' feet?

As we study God's word and start to understand the kindness that He shows us, we will be able to apply it to our lives as well.

Jesus encourages us to follow His lead and support one another.

He sets an example for us to follow. He washed feet; He fed thousands of people. He visited the sick, and even spent time with people that nobody else wanted to spend time with!

We need to work on following God's example by examining our hearts. The contents of our hearts spill out into our words and actions.

Do you have compassion for those around you and want to help them, or are you always worried about yourself and how to make yourself happy?

Sometimes it is hard to put others first, and it doesn't come easy. If you are struggling to show kindness, you can ask God to change your heart. He's always faithful to help.

~Time To Pray~

Lord, please help me to love people. Work in my
heart and make it tender and compassionate so that
I can do your work and help others the way you want
me to! Thank you for being such a great example
of kindness to me, help me to be just like You!
Amen.

KINDNESS CONVERSATIONS

Do you think **Jesus is kind?**

What is one thing you could do today to
show someone **kindness?**

What is one thing that someone has done for
you recently to **show kindness?**

3 Kind To Everyone

"[35] But love your enemies, do good to them, and lend to them without expecting to get anything back. Then your reward will be great, and you will be children of the Most High, because he is kind to the ungrateful and wicked."
Luke 6:35

Has anyone ever been unkind to you?
Did they call you a mean name, take your toy, or even push you down?
How did you react?
Did you shove them back?
Or did you just let it go and walk away?

Jesus asks us to love those who aren't easy to love. He wants us to be kind to them. And you know what? He even wants us to be kind and not expect them to be kind back! Wow.

Do you think that's possible?
I do!

You can do it with God's help. He won't ever ask you to do something that you can't do.

Jesus also asks us to lend to others without expecting to get anything back. If a buddy at school forgets his eraser, you lend him yours, and then he forgets to give it back, what should you do?

Does he owe you one?
Should you always remind him that he took your eraser?
No!

People are more valuable than possessions, and we need to start putting them first. Hopefully, your buddy will remember you lent him that eraser and give it back, but if not, that's okay.

Jesus will help you forget about it, and He will bless you for blessing your friend.

The next time someone is unkind to you, try your very best to be kind anyway. Smile big and say, "It's okay!" or just walk away. I'll bet they'll be surprised by your reaction and change their attitude.

If not, that's also okay because God will see your kindness, and that is what really matters.

~Time To Pray~

Lord, thank you for giving me the strength to do hard things. Being kind to people who are not kind to me will not be easy, but I know that I can do it because I have Your help! Please help me be kind to everyone today!
Amen.

KINDNESS CONVERSATIONS

On a separate piece of paper, **list three (3) ways** that you could show someone that they're more important than your possessions.
(If you can't write, just say it!)

4 Kindness Benefits You

"[17] Those who are kind benefit themselves, but the cruel bring ruin on themselves."
Proverbs 11:17

Do you think being kind makes you feel good or feel bad?
Yes, it makes you feel great!

God blesses us when we are kind to others. I have another couple of questions:

How do you feel when you've been cruel or mean to somebody?
Do you get an icky feeling in your tummy or feel sad?
I do too.

Do you know why? God created us to love one another, so when we are unkind, our heart knows it. It's imperative to listen to God and his Holy Spirit when he tells us what is right or wrong and what is kind or unkind.

That feeling you get after you aren't nice to someone is probably the Holy Spirit telling you that it wasn't okay.

And when you get a warm, fuzzy feeling after you've done something nice for someone, be sure to thank Jesus for showing you how to be kind!

In what ways do you think the Holy Spirit speaks to us?

He speaks to us through the Bible, our parents, the little feelings we get when we do something right or something wrong, and he will even talk to you through this study.

Make sure you pay close attention and always try to do what Jesus tells you to do!

~Time To Pray~

Lord, thank you for your Holy Spirit. Teach me to pay attention when He is speaking to me and showing me right from wrong. Help me always to do my very best for You!
Amen.

KINDNESS CONVERSATIONS

Have you done anything **kind for someone** recently?

Describe **how you felt** when you did that.

Can you think of **something you could do or say** to make **someone feel loved** today?

"[16] You did not choose me, but I chose you and appointed you so that you might go and bear fruit—fruit that will last—and so that whatever you ask in my name the Father will give you."
John 15:16

When you are a Christian and believe in what the Bible says, it's always important to try and do what Jesus tells us through His words in the Bible. We are learning that he wants us to be kind and compassionate.

We have been chosen, called, and anointed to be His disciples and tell others about Him!

Kindness can look like lots of different things! It can be a nice compliment to someone, a sweet smile, an act of service like doing a chore for your parents, or sharing a toy with your brother or sister.

There are lots of ways to show kindness!

Sometimes it's not easy. Sometimes it's tough! But we are God's chosen ones. He chose us to be His. And it is our job to show others who God is. God is kind, and if we are kind, also, people will see Him in you and begin to understand who He is.

That's a big responsibility, but you can do it.
God is on your side!

~Time To Pray~

Lord, thank you for choosing me! Please help me to be kind and have a compassionate heart as You do. I want to show people that I love you and to show them how amazing You are! Keep showing me how to be more and more like You.
Amen!

KINDNESS CONVERSATIONS

Do you think that **when you're kind to someone, it makes them feel loved?**

Do **you feel loved** when someone is **kind** to you, or does **something special** for you?

What is something you did once that was **not** very **kind?**

What is **something that you could say** to make them **feel better?**

"[4] Love is patient, love is kind. It does not envy, it does not boast, it is not proud. [5] It does not dishonor others, it is not self-seeking, it is not easily angered, it keeps no record of wrongs."
1 Corinthians 13:4-5

Love is kind.
What do you think that means?

God wants us to love others by showing them kindness.

What are some ways you can show kindness to others?

When I think of kindness, I picture someone sharing something with a friend or a sibling, or giving a compliment such as: "I love your shoes!" OR "I think you're nice!"

Kindness is helping someone up when they fall, cheering him or her up when they're sad, or giving someone a great, big, bear hug!

This Bible verse also shows us some behaviors that *aren't* kind. Love doesn't boast or brag; love isn't thinking you're better than someone else, love isn't rude or grouchy, and it doesn't count how many times someone has wronged you.

Love is to forgive others.

Lets try and show people love today by being kind, patient, compassionate, and sweet!

I'll bet it will put a smile on someone's face, and Jesus will be so proud of you!

~Time To Pray~

Lord, please help me be kind today! I want to open up my heart and mind so that I can hear You speak to me and show me ways for me to be kind to others! I want to make You proud, Jesus. Thank you for Your gift of kindness. **Amen.**

KINDNESS CONVERSATIONS

Who should you **be kind to?**

What are some **kind things** you could say to someone?

What should you do if you hear a kid at school say something unkind to another kid?

7 It Takes Work

"[5] For this very reason, make every effort to add to your faith goodness; and to goodness, knowledge; [6] and to knowledge, self-control; and to self-control, perseverance; and to perseverance, godliness; [7] and to godliness, mutual affection; and to mutual affection, love."
2 Peter 1:5-7

When we become Christians, our hearts are washed clean. As white as snow! But, we still have to work hard to become more and more like Jesus.

We are so lucky to have the Bible, a book that we can go to that teaches us how to be like Him. It gives us all the answers we need to know.

Jesus wants us to work hard to be good, to have self-control, and to be kind!

Being kind is one way we can love Jesus, other people, and even ourselves.

Did you do something kind for someone recently?
If you did, great job!

Jesus wants to help you to be more kind and loving to others. Make sure you ask him for help!

~Time To Pray~

Jesus, thank you for dying on the cross and washing me clean. Thank you for forgiving my sins. Help me to honor you today by loving others and showing them kindness, just as You have done for me! Bless the rest of my day, and help me to be kind!
Amen.

KINDNESS CONVERSATIONS

Should you only **be kind** when you're at home with your family?

Should you be kind while you're **at school and church?**

We should **always be kind,** so what should you do if you're at a friend's house and their mom makes a dinner that you don't like?

8 The Golden Rule

"[31] Do to others as you would have
them do to you."
Luke 6:31

This Bible verse is so important. If we apply it to our lives daily, we would surely achieve our goal of being more kind.

These special words in the Bible are referred to as ***The Golden Rule*** *and are words that we should keep in our hearts and always remember.*

Jesus is telling us to treat other people exactly how we would want them to treat us.

How do you like people to treat you?

I like it when people listen to me, share with me, treat me respectfully, and are honest and kind!

Do you think others would like to be treated that way, too?
Yes!

We all want to be treated kindly, so let's learn to treat others as we want to be treated! God will always be faithful to tell us how he wants us to live and how to act.

We just need to listen.

~Time To Pray~

Thank you, Lord, for being so patient with me and teaching me how to be kind. Thank you for teaching me how to love others. Help me always to treat others the way that I want to be treated. I pray that you would show me the ways that I can treat others kindly today!
Amen.

KINDNESS CONVERSATIONS

If you **have siblings,** are you **always kind to them?**

Do you want them **always to be kind to you?**

What should you do when your little brother or sister plays with your brand-new toy and breaks it?

If you had **two (2)** pieces of candy and your sister or brother didn't have any, **what would be the kind thing to do?**

"[27] He answered, " 'Love the Lord your God with all your heart and with all your soul and with all your strength and with all your mind'; and, 'Love your neighbor as yourself.'"
Luke 10:27

Have you ever heard the story in the Bible of the Good Samaritan?

It's one of the **greatest parables**, and it teaches us about kindness. A parable is a simple story used to teach a lesson, as told by Jesus in the Gospels.

Jesus uses this parable to teach us about loving your neighbor as you love yourself.

The story describes a man who was walking down the street and suddenly was robbed and beaten! Lots of people just walked right by him and didn't even help him.

Finally, a kind man – The Good Samaritan - stopped to help him. The Good Samaritan put the hurt man on his donkey and brought him somewhere to get care, which he paid for with his own money. He felt compassion for him.

Isn't that a great example of somebody showing kindness?

Maybe the man imagined that if this had been him, he would have wanted someone to stop and help! He must have known about the Golden Rule!

Would you have stopped and helped him?
Even though he was dirty?

We need to continue learning how to love people like we want to be loved and how Jesus loves us!

Sometimes it isn't easy, but God will always be there to help us!

~Time To Pray~

Lord, I want to be like the Good Samaritan in the Bible. Please, show me how to have compassion and be kind to others like he did. Help me always to be looking for ways to be kind to others!
Amen.

KINDNESS CONVERSATIONS

If you saw a group of kids picking on another kid
on the playground, **what should you do?**

What would be the best thing to do
if you saw someone drop a **ten (10)** dollar bill
on the ground without knowing they did it?

If you were at the park and
you noticed some garbage lying on the ground,
what could you do to be helpful and kind?

10 Mind Of Christ

"[5] May the God who gives endurance and encouragement give you the same attitude of mind toward each other that Christ Jesus had,"
Romans 15:5

What attitude of mind did Christ have?
And what does it even mean to have the mind of Christ?

When Christians have the mind of Christ, it means that they understand that His plan for the world is to bring glory to God and to teach others about Him.

When we have the mind of Christ, we are always trying to show others who God is.

What is a good way to show people who God is?

One way is through our actions. Since Jesus is kind and compassionate, we need to show kindness and compassion to others.

When you go out of your way to be kind to someone, often, they are surprised. It gets their attention. And they wonder what is different about you.

They see Jesus in you.

If they don't know about Jesus, they begin to understand a little bit about who Jesus is.

He is so kind!

Do you understand why it's important to have the mind of Christ and to treat each other with kindness?

Let's pray for God's help.

~Time To Pray~

Lord, I thank you for being so loving and compassionate. I pray that if there are people in my life that don't know about you that you would allow me to show them compassion and kindness. Even though I'm small, I pray that you would use me to show your great work, Lord! I am ready!
Amen.

KINDNESS CONVERSATIONS

Do you think that **you're too young** for **Jesus** to use you?

Do you want to **help Jesus** by showing and **telling others who He is?**

What is **something that you could do** for someone today that would **show them Jesus' love?**

"[18] Dear children, let us not love with words or speech but with actions and in truth."
1 John 3:18

The words "I love you" are so important to say to the people who are special to you!

Even though they probably already know, it's still important to say it!

What else can we do to show someone we love them?
Can we show them through our actions?
Yes, we can!

Jesus says it's essential to not only love with words but also with actions!

What is something that you could do for your mom, dad, sister, brother, or even a friend today to show them kindness and display how much you love them?

You could hold the door open for someone, share a toy with a friend, make someone else's bed, or just give someone a big hug!

Challenge yourself to show kindness to someone you love today, and be sure to stick around to see them smile!

~Time To Pray~

Jesus, thank you for putting people in my life who love me. I pray that you would show me ways to express my love to them today! Help me to be kind, compassionate, and loving to those around me!
Amen.

KINDNESS CONVERSATIONS

Are you going **to try hard today** to show your friends and family that **you love them?**

Today, **a unique way to show kindness** will be to do an extra chore for your parent. Can you imagine **how happy they'll be?**

12 Put Others First

"[3] Do nothing out of selfish ambition or vain conceit. Rather, in humility value others above yourselves, [4] not looking to your own interests but each of you to the interests of the others."
Philippians 2:3-4

Have you ever gotten into a disagreement with a friend over what game you were going to play?
Have you ever told someone that you're better at something than they are?
What about grabbing the biggest piece of cake and leaving the smaller ones for everyone else?

We are all sinners by nature, and we have all been selfish in our lives.

God is always faithful to forgive us.

Jesus wants us to put others first. He wants us to let our friends choose the game, tell someone that they're great at something, and let them eat the big piece of cake! It's okay to play games that you like.

Just make sure you're playing games that your friends like, too!

When we put others first, Jesus always makes sure that we get taken care of, as well. You'll notice that when you look out for others, it will make you feel good, too!

~Time To Pray~

God, today I learned that You want me to put others first. That sounds kind of hard. I pray that you would give me the strength to be kind to others and put their needs before mine. I know that You will bless me for it. **Amen**.

KINDNESS CONVERSATIONS

What would you do if your friend came over and asked if he could ride your brand-new bike?

If there were only **two (2)** cookies left and you knew your sister wanted one too, **should you eat them both?**

If you knew that your grandma wasn't feeling well and you went over to her house and saw that the house was a little messy, **what is something that you could do to show kindness and help her out?**

"[8] Above all, love each other deeply, because love covers over a multitude of sins."
1 Peter 4:8

What do you think this Bible verse means?
Do you think it means that being kind makes our sins go away?
No!

Only Jesus can get rid of our sins. He died on the cross a long time ago to cover the sins that we hadn't even done yet.

Before we were even born!
Wow!

Jesus wants you to know that the more that you love people and show them kindness, the easier it becomes. It becomes a habit - a life-style. You find yourself thinking of more and more ways to show people kindness.

When we are completely immersed in loving other people and trying to spread kindness, we have less time to think about sinning.

We are so focused on loving other people for Jesus that we don't even want to sin. Isn't that cool?

We are not perfect and never will be.

But God loves us anyway! We just need to try our best and always ask him for help.

~Time To Pray ~

Lord, I pray that You would help me to be so focused on being kind to those around me that the devil won't be able to convince me to sin. Holy Spirit, turn my heart towards God. Jesus, forgive my sins. I thank You because I always can come to You for encouragement and forgiveness!
Amen.

KINDNESS CONVERSATIONS

Have you ever **made the mistake** of treating someone unkindly?

Do you think **Jesus forgave you** for being unkind to others?
*Hint. **The answer is 'absolutely'!**

What **act of kindness** could you do for a friend today?

"[35] In everything I did, I showed you that by this kind of hard work we must help the weak, remembering the words the Lord Jesus himself said: 'It is more blessed to give than to receive.'"
Acts 20:35

Do you enjoy picking out gifts for others?

It's so rewarding to watch them open it, see their eyes light up, and to see them smile!

Receiving gifts is a lot of fun, too, isn't it?

God wants us to find joy in giving to others! He says that it's better to give than to receive.

What are some ways that you can put others before yourself?

You could share one of your snacks at snack-time, draw a picture for someone special, or maybe pick a flower for your mom or dad. Those acts of kindness would put a smile on someone's face, wouldn't they?

Let's try and change our focus from always wanting something new and thinking about what we are going to get; instead, let's try to always think about how we can give to others and show kindness to them!

Jesus will surely bless us as we learn to give rather than receive.

~Time To Pray~

Jesus, thank you for giving me the ultimate gift: Dying on the cross for me. I want to learn to give to others. Please be with me as I show kindness to others and show me new ways to bless them! I am so fortunate to have Your guidance!
Amen.

KINDNESS CONVERSATIONS

When was the last time you gave someone **a gift?**

How did it **make you feel?**

How do you think it **made them feel?**

Today, **I challenge you** to give someone a small gift. Something simple such as;
pick your mom a flower, draw your dad a picture, or write a special note for a friend!

"[8] Finally, all of you, be like-minded, be sympathetic, love one another, be compassionate and humble."
1 Peter 3:8

Kindness is contagious!

Do you know what the word 'contagious' means?

The definition is 'an emotion, feeling, or attitude that is likely to spread to and affect others.'

It means that when someone shows an act of kindness to someone else, that person most likely will show kindness to someone too!

Sometimes, the kind acts will continue on and on and bless more and more people!

Here's a fun example: it's very common for someone to go through a fast-food drive-through or a coffee stand, and they'll pay for the person's order in the car behind them.

Quite often, that person will feel so blessed and will then pay for the person behind them, and the chain of kindness will continue on and on.

Don't you love that?
Has that ever happened to your mom, dad,
or someone you know before?

Let's challenge ourselves to start a chain of kindness today!

~Time To Pray~

Jesus, today I pray that You would allow me to spread kindness to others. Open my eyes and heart so that I can hear Your voice prompting me throughout the day as you show me how to be kind, compassionate, and loving!
Amen.

KINDNESS CONVERSATIONS

If you could do **one kind act** for one person in the world, **who** would it be, and **what would you do?**

If you saw an **older adult** at the store struggling to lift something heavy into their shopping cart, **what could you do to help?**

Why is it important to do **kind things for others?**

"[8] He has shown you, O mortal, what is good.
And what does the Lord require of you?
To act justly and to love mercy
and to walk humbly with your God."
Micah 6:8

There was a man named Micah who lived a very long time ago. **He was a prophet.**

A prophet is someone who loves God and receives special instruction from God so that they can tell people what God wants from them.

In those days, people would bring offerings to the priests as gifts for God. They would bring things like wheat, barley, sheep, or bulls.

The people asked Micah what they should bring to God that would show him the most gratitude. Then, God spoke to Micah and told him to tell the people that he didn't want any gift.

God has everything he needs!

He instructed Micah to tell the people that he wanted them to do justly, love mercy, and walk humbly with God!

Do you know what the word "Just" means?

It means to be fair. To love mercy means to love being kind to people. Walking humbly with God means to be close to Him and to understand that he is God, and we are not. We are not better than anyone else. Say these words with me and memorize them:

- ***Do justly,***
- ***Love mercy,***
- ***Walk humbly with God.***

Great job!

~Time To Pray~

Jesus, thank you for being so patient with me as I learn to do justly, love mercy, and walk humbly with You. I know that I'm never going to be perfect, and I thank You for Your Grace and forgiveness. Help me to do my best. Cleanse my heart and make me more like You. **Amen.**

KINDNESS CONVERSATIONS

Who should you **be kind** to?

How can you **be kind at home?**

What is one thing you could do to **show kindness to your sibling** today?

"[29] Do not let any unwholesome talk come out of your mouths, but only what is helpful for building others up according to their needs, that it may benefit those who listen."
Ephesians 4:29

Have you ever heard somebody speak words that weren't very kind?

Maybe you have even said something unkind to someone!

Do you know who loves it when we say mean things?
The devil.

He is the father of lies. He wants us to tear each other down and make each other feel bad. Luckily, we have Jesus and His words in the Bible to help us fight against Satan's lies.

Our words are very powerful. The words that come from the Bible are words of love and kindness and can fight against Satan's darkness.

The Bible tells us to encourage one another and build each other up!

It's very important that we watch our words and only speak life to those around us!

Sometimes, we don't' know the troubles that those around us are facing. If someone was having a terrible day and you said something unkind to them, do you think they would feel even worse? Yes, most likely they would.

It's essential to always be kind.

~Time To Pray~

Jesus, I know that You are more powerful than the devil and that I do not need to be afraid. I know that it's important for me to always make sure I'm speaking life-giving words and not allowing Satan to lie to me. Help me to see the truth and recognize when my thoughts and actions are not from You. Help me to be kind and to build others up with my words! **Amen.**

KINDNESS CONVERSATIONS

What should you do if one of your friends said something mean to someone else?

When your parent asks you to **get ready for bed,** but you're right in the middle of playing a game, **what would be the kind thing to do?**

How should you respond?

18 Build Each Other Up

"[2] Each of us should please our neighbors for their good, to build them up."
Romans 15:2

One day, a little girl named Annie was on the school playground with her best friend Kara when another girl walked up to them and asked if she could play.

Annie was just about to say "yes" when Kara grabbed her arm and pulled her away!

"That girl is weird, and I don't want to play with her," whispered Kara.

Annie was surprised by her friend. She took a second to think about how to respond.

Annie knew that Jesus wanted her to love everyone and treat them how she would want to be treated.

But she also didn't want to embarrass Kara.

What would you do in this situation?
Do you want to know what Annie did?

She gently laid her hand on Kara's arm and said, "Kara, Jesus wants us to be kind to others. Wouldn't you be sad if someone didn't want to play with you?"

Kara looked down at her feet, looking very guilty.

Annie continued, "We need to do what Jesus says and do what's right."

Kara smiled and said, "You're right Annie, I'm sorry. Let's go get her so we can all play together."

Have you ever been in a situation like this?

Let's be like Annie and always try to do what is right, even if we are uncomfortable. God will help you and give you the courage!

~Time To Pray~

Lord, please give me the courage to always stand up and do what is right. I want to build people up and make them feel good. I want to help people obey You and follow Your commands. Help me lead with love and kindness.
Amen.

KINDNESS CONVERSATIONS

Have you ever had someone **leave you out** before?

Have you ever **been tempted** to leave someone out?

Why is it important to **make sure that you're not making someone feel left out?**

19 Never Stop Being Kind

"[13] And as for you, brothers and sisters, never tire of doing what is good.."
2 Thessalonians 3:13

Can you think of any examples of someone who has gotten tired of doing good?

Here's one example: Let's say you left out all of your brand-new markers with no lids on them!

What would happen to them?
Would they dry up?
Yes, they would!

So, what could happen if we got tired of doing good?
We could get all dried up!

Jesus needs us to work hard and to always spread love and kindness to those around us.

Remember how we learned about spreading kindness and that when we are kind to someone, they are kind to someone else, and it creates a kindness chain?

If we decided to stop being kind, there would be so many people affected by that.

You and your kindness matter!

One person can make a big difference in God's kingdom, so make sure that you're always on guard, always listening to the Holy Spirit, and always being kind!

~Time To Pray~

Jesus, thank you for helping me not to be idle and lazy, growing tired of being kind. Help me always to be looking for a way to bless someone with love and kindness! Use me to expand Your kingdom and spread kindness to those who need it. I love You, Lord!
Amen.

KINDNESS CONVERSATIONS

Do you believe **kindness is contagious?**

Why?

On a separate sheet of paper, **write down all the words** you can make using the letters in the word **KINDNESS.**
(If you can't write, just say it!)

20 United In Christ

"[8] Finally, all of you, be like-minded, be sympathetic, love one another, be compassionate and humble."
1 Peter 3:8

What do you think it means to be "like-minded"?

These words are referring to people who all have the mind of Christ. People who think like Jesus!

Do you want to have the mind of Christ?
Let's go over some ways that we can all be like-minded.

We can learn to take our thoughts captive and make sure we always have good ones, thoughts that are always pleasing to Jesus.

We can and should read our Bibles and keep His words in our hearts by memorizing scriptures, and we can learn to have compassion, love, and kindness for others.

Are you going to be always perfect?
No!

Is Jesus going to be always there to help you?
Yes!

It's essential to try to do your best in pleasing our God. He is so faithful to help us and guide us. We are just so lucky to have Jesus!

Make this day count. Go out and practice having a mind like Christ.

You can do it!

~Time To Pray~

Lord, today I learned what it means to have the mind of Christ. That is a huge task! I want to do my best and be like You. Will You please help me? I want to learn to be compassionate, humble, and kind, and I know that I can do it with Your help. Thank you, Jesus! **Amen.**

KINDNESS CONVERSATIONS

What does it mean to **take your thoughts** captive?

Why is it important to **read our Bible?**

When you're having a hard time **being kind,** what is something that you can do to **help get back on track?**

"[9]This is what the Lord Almighty said: 'Administer true justice; show mercy and compassion to one another."
Zechariah 7:9

There are so many verses in the Bible about being kind and showing compassion to those around us.

It means that God feels that kindness it's pretty important, don't you think?
I do!

We've been learning about what kindness means for quite a while now.

Do you feel like God is changing your heart and helping you be compassionate to others?
What are some ways you've shown kindness lately?
Do you have any examples of how others have been kind to you?

Sometimes it's not easy to be kind, is it? When we are having a bad day, or didn't get much sleep the night before, or feel disappointed about something, we may not act like our best self.

In our moments of weakness, we sometimes say or do unkind things. We are just humans, after all!

If you've been unkind to someone, what do you think Jesus would want you to do? Apologize?
Yes!

That would be the best thing to do. You both will feel so much better, and it will be so pleasing to the Lord.

~Time To Pray~

Lord, thank you for teaching me kindness. I know that one of the best ways to love people is to be kind to them. You know that I'm not perfect, and I pray that if there is anything unkind I have done to someone, that you would show me so that I can apologize and make things better. Thank you, Jesus!
Amen.

KINDNESS CONVERSATIONS

How do you feel that you're doing as far as **being more kind?**

Think of a time recently that you did something kind for someone and **draw a picture** of it on a separate piece of paper!

22 Let The Children Come

"[7] in order that in the coming ages he might show the incomparable riches of his grace, expressed in his kindness to us in Christ Jesus."
Ephesians 2:7

Jesus is a perfect example of kindness.

If you ever find yourself wondering what kindness means, all you have to do is open your Bible! There are many stories in there about Jesus showing kindness.

Did you ever read about when Jesus was hanging out with his disciples, and a group of children came up and wanted to see Him?

The disciples tried to send the children away, but Jesus said, ***"Let the little children come!"*** He welcomed them and even blessed them with His hands.

Jesus is so kind and loving.
We need to make it our goal to be like Jesus!
Remember to pray and ask him for help!

Proverbs 3:6 says, "In all ways acknowledge him and he will direct your paths." That means He will help you to do the right thing.

You are never alone.

When times get hard, and you have trouble being kind, God will help you. Remember, all it takes is a quick conversation with Him. Ask him to change your heart and give you compassion.

Never forget that you have His help!

~Time To Pray~

Lord, thank you for being such a fantastic example of loving-kindness. I pray that You would continue to help me love people and show them compassion and kindness. Continue to give me opportunities that will help me grow. I want to be like You, Jesus. Make me more and more like You every day! **Amen.**

KINDNESS CONVERSATIONS

What are some **actions that show kindness?**

What are some **words that show kindness?**

If everyone in the world did **one kind thing every day,** what do you think the world would look like?

23

Be Kind To You!

"[14] I praise you because I am fearfully and
wonderfully made;
your works are wonderful,
I know that full well."
Psalms 139:14

I think we all can agree that God's works are wonderful, can't we?

Did God make you?
That means you must be wonderful, doesn't it?

Not only is it important to be kind to others, but it is also important to be kind to yourself.

It's essential to love yourself, not in a proud or boastful sort of way, but in a Godly, respectful way.

God created you in His image!

You are fearfully and wonderfully made! God doesn't make mistakes. He made you on purpose.

Wow!

Do you have any ideas of how you can be kind to yourself? Let's list a few ways:

1. You can spend time praying every day so that you can grow to be more like Jesus,
2. You can put healthy food in your body,
3. You can watch shows and listen to music that is pleasing to the Lord,
4. You can think good thoughts about yourself!

It's so important to be kind to yourself and treat yourself well. If you're healthy and thriving, then you'll be able to be kind to others even more.

Make sure you are kind to yourself today!

~Time To Pray~

Lord, thank You for making me in Your image. Your works are wonderful, and I know that very well. Please help me be kind to myself. Help me to think kind and positive thoughts about myself and to give myself Grace when I make mistakes.
I love You, Jesus.
Amen.

KINDNESS CONVERSATIONS

On a separate piece of paper, write down
six (6) things that you **love about yourself**
(If you can't write, just say it!)

"[10] Be devoted to one another in love. Honor one another above yourselves."
Romans 12:10

Sometimes being kind is hard.

Sometimes being kind means giving up something that you like so that someone in need can have it. Here's an example of a little girl who put someone else first:

Her name was Jane, and she was sitting at the lunch table at school. Jane was excited to eat the leftover pizza her mom had packed her. Pizza was her very favorite food.

She was just about to take a bite when she noticed her friend Grace didn't have lunch and wasn't eating!

Jane got closer to her friend and asked her why she didn't have lunch, to which Grace answered: "I forgot mine at home, and now I don't have anything to eat." As Grace said this, a tear slipped from her eye.

Jane looked at her pizza, and then at her teary-eyed friend. She had two huge slices, so she knew, in her heart, what God wanted her to do.

She reached over, took one of her slices, and handed it over to Grace. Grace's face lit up. She was so happy and relieved!

Jane felt very happy because she knew that she was pleasing the Lord.

How remarkable is that story! What a great example of kindness and Godly sacrifice!

Let's continue to try our hardest to be kind and please the Lord even when it means putting others before ourselves! ***God will reward us greatly.***

~Time To Pray~

Lord, I thank You for giving me the strength to put others before myself. I pray that You would give me opportunities to show kindness. When I'm in a situation where I can bless someone by giving them something of mine, I pray that You'd help me to be selfless and obedient to You at that moment.
Thank you, Lord.
Amen.

KINDNESS CONVERSATIONS

What are **five (5)** things that you can do to **help at home today?**

25 Kind To The Poor

"[17] Whoever is kind to the poor lends to the Lord,
and he will reward them for
what they have done."
Proverbs 19:17

There is a story in the Bible of a man named Zacchaeus. He was a wealthy tax collector, and he wasn't a sincere man. He stole money from a lot of people. One day he got to meet Jesus in real life!

From that moment on, his life was completely changed. His heart was changed because the Holy Spirit spoke to him and showed him how to be kind.

He gave half of his possessions to the poor, and he paid back everyone he stole from.

That's what happens when we allow Jesus to rule our lives.

He transforms our hearts and minds and helps us to be kind and to give to the poor when they are in need, just like Zacchaeus did!

Have you ever had the chance to give to someone in need? Maybe you gave a toy to a child who didn't have many toys, or your family helped feed someone who didn't have money to buy groceries!

Throughout your life, God will provide ways that you can help people in need; you just need to keep your heart and eyes open and be ready!

~Time To Pray~

Dear Lord, I thank You for the fantastic stories in the Bible that we can learn from. Please help me to be gracious and kind whenever I see someone in need. Help me to put other people first and trust that You will take care of my needs! **Amen**.

KINDNESS CONVERSATIONS

Have you ever **helped someone less fortunate than you?**

You can **donate things** that you own to other kids in need. Take some time today to fill a bag and **ask your mom to help you** donate it!

26 Let Your Light Shine

"[16] In the same way, let your light shine before others, that they may see your good deeds and glorify your Father in heaven."
Matthew 5:16

What happens when you try and turn on a flashlight that doesn't have any batteries in it?
Does it work?
Does it shine?
No.

How do you think you could make the flashlight work?
You have to clean out the inside of it and insert batteries for it to work correctly!

Now, think about the Bible verse in this lesson. It says Jesus wants us to shine our light.

What do you think that means?

Jesus wants to clean us of all our sins and give us the Holy Spirit to make us shine. He wants our actions and words to reflect Him.

Jesus wants people to see Him in us. He wants our words to be compassionate and our actions to be kind.

Jesus says that when others see your good deeds, they will know that there is something different about you and know that Jesus is in You.

He wants us to love others just as He loves us!

~Time To Pray~

Thank you, Lord, for sending Your Holy Spirit to lead me and guide me. It's not always easy to show others kindness and compassion, but I know that You have equipped me with the tools that I need to be able to do it. Please help me to let my light shine so that others may see You and glorify Your name, Jesus!
Amen.

KINDNESS CONVERSATIONS

If you had a lot of money and could use it to **bless someone** else, **what would you do?**

Do you need to have a lot of money to **be able to bless someone?**

What is one small thing that you could do right now to **make someone smile?**

"[3] Because your love is better than life,
my lips will glorify you."
Psalms 63:3

Sometimes it's hard to be kind. Sometimes you just aren't in the mood.

Does that mean that you should just give up and not try?
No, it doesn't.

I love the Bible verse that we learned today. A man of God named David from the Bible wrote it while he was stuck in the wilderness!

He was probably hungry, tired, and a little afraid, yet he was still praising the Lord and doing what God wanted him to do.

David said that the Lord's loving kindness is better than life itself.
He loved God so much.

The Bible says he longed for God and thought about Him all of the time.

Do you feel like you think about God all of the time?
That is what He wants from us.

He wants us always to be thinking about His words, and He wants us to talk to Him! He wants us to pray.

What is praying?
It's just talking to God!

You can talk to Him as if He is right in the room with you because He can hear you! As we grow in our prayer life and learn to speak with Jesus, He helps us and teaches us.

He will help you as you're on your journey to being more kind.
Aren't you glad you have his help?

~Time To Pray~

Lord, I want to be like David in the Bible, always
thinking about You and talking to You. Help me to be
kind and loving even when my situation isn't perfect.
As I learn to pray and deepen my relationship with You,
I pray that Your spirit would move in me and change
me. Make me a strong leader for Your kingdom!
Thank you, Jesus!
Amen.

KINDNESS CONVERSATIONS

Can you **think of a time** when it was tough for you to be kind?

Who is **the kindest person** you know?

What is **the kindest thing you've ever seen** someone do?

28 Love Your Enemies

"[43] You have heard that it was said, 'Love your neighbor and hate your enemy.' [44] But I tell you, love your enemies and pray for those who persecute you,"
Matthew 5:43-44

What do you think of when you see a heart?
When I see a heart, I think of love.

Who do you love? Do you love your parents and grandparents? How about your brothers or sisters? You probably love your best friends, also!

It's easy to love these people because they love us, too!

Has anyone ever been mean to you? Has someone pushed you over on the playground, called you a mean name, or left you out? Do you feel love for those people?

Do you think we are supposed to love people who aren't kind to us?
Yes, Jesus tells us to love even our enemies.
But how?
That sounds hard!

Jesus says we need to love our enemies and PRAY for them! Wow! He says that when we love our enemies, we are acting like children of God.

We can't only love the people who are kind to us. What's so special about that? Everyone does that! What is really special is when you are kind to those who aren't easy to be kind to.

That's when you'll see God's blessings.

~Time To Pray~

Father, it is easy to love my family and friends, but it isn't as easy loving people who aren't kind to me. Please help me to show love to those who are hard to love so that they will see You in me! I pray that You would use me to draw them closer to You, Jesus!
Amen.

KINDNESS CONVERSATIONS

Is there anyone in your life who makes it **challenging to be kind to them?**

What is something that you could do to **show them kindness,** even when you don't feel like it?

Do you think that people who act mean all the time can change and **become kinder?**

"[27] "But to you who are listening I say: Love your enemies, do good to those who hate you, [28] bless those who curse you, pray for those who mistreat you."
Luke 6:27-28

There are a lot of verses in the Bible that tell us to love our enemies. **Jesus feels that it's really important**. The rest of this Bible verse says that if someone slaps your face, you need to turn the other cheek!

What does that mean?
Is Jesus saying that when someone slaps you
that you should hit him or her back?
No, He is saying that you should turn your other cheek.

Because you are a child and not yet an adult, **Jesus would want you to tell a parent if this happens to you.**

What he is also saying is that you shouldn't try and harm them back. If somebody hurts you, they will be shocked if you choose to be kind in return!

*They'll wonder what is different about you,
and you can tell them about Jesus!*

Jesus also says that if somebody takes your coat, you should give him or her your shirt, too! He wants us to be kind, gracious and giving.

Jesus wants us to always put other people's feelings above our own.

He says to do unto others, as we would want them to do unto us.

***The Golden Rule*.**

Jesus knows this isn't easy, but He offers his Holy Spirit to help and guide us. **He knows you can do it!**

~Time To Pray~

Thank you, Jesus, for giving me Your Holy Spirit to
help me in times of trouble. I pray that You would help
me to be kind to those who aren't kind to me. Help me
to trust You and know that You are always looking out
for me and keeping me from harm. I know that if I put
others above myself that You will take care of me.
Thank you, Lord!
Amen.

KINDNESS CONVERSATIONS

If you were playing on the playground and someone ran by and pushed you over, **would it be okay to chase after them and push them back?**

What should you do if your brother calls you a mean, and it makes you angry?

"[35] But love your enemies, do good to them, and lend to them without expecting to get anything back. Then your reward will be great, and you will be children of the Most High, because he is kind to the ungrateful and wicked. [36] Be merciful, just as your Father is merciful."
Luke 6:35-36

We are continuing our study in the chapter of Luke today because there is just so much good stuff to learn!

In the last lesson, we talked about how Jesus wants us to turn the other cheek when someone is unkind to us. We have talked about how Jesus wants us to pray for our enemies.

This verse talks about how Jesus wants us to lend out our belongings and not expect to get them back!
Does that sound hard, or what?

Jesus says, in Luke, that if we do these things, our reward will be great, and we will be called His children!

Do you think that Jesus would expect you to be
kind to others if He didn't do so himself?
No way!

The Bible says that Jesus is kind to the ungrateful and wicked.

Jesus is merciful.

What does merciful mean? Being merciful is when you show compassion and forgiveness to someone who should be punished.

Be merciful just as your Father is merciful.

~Time To Pray~

Jesus, I want to be merciful. I want to be compassionate and kind to others. Please help me lay down my desires so that I can focus on others and their needs. Thank you for calling me Your child. Help me to be grateful for all the things You have given me and to share them with others willingly.
In Jesus' mighty name, we pray!
Amen.

KINDNESS CONVERSATIONS

Do you think that **everyone can learn to be kind?**

Is it harder to **be kind when others are watching** or when they aren't?

Should we be kind even when there aren't a lot of people around?

"[32] Be kind and compassionate to one another, forgiving each other, just as in Christ God forgave you."
Ephesians 4:32

Forgiveness.
What does that mean?
Have you ever been forgiven?

I'm sure your parents or grandparents have forgiven you for disobeying or sinning.

We all have sinned!

Do you know what was the most significant and important time that someone forgave you in your life? It was when Jesus died on the cross a long, long time ago.

He was doing it to forgive your sins even
though you weren't even born yet!
That's how much He loves you!

If Jesus can forgive you before you have even sinned, then you can forgive someone *after* they have hurt you or sinned against you.

Can you think of an example of someone who has hurt you or hurt your feelings lately? Take a moment to think of something…

If the Lord showed you something just now, then He wants you to forgive that person. Let's pray and ask Jesus to help us forgive those who have been unkind to us.

~Time To Pray~

Father God, I know that being angry with someone who hasn't been kind to me isn't good for me. Please help me to forgive them even though they don't deserve it. I know that I didn't deserve You dying on the cross for my sins, and because of that, I know I can also forgive. Thank you for Your cross, Lord!
Amen.

KINDNESS CONVERSATIONS

Does **Jesus** ever get tired of **forgiving us?**

Is there a limit on how many times **we are supposed to forgive others?**

Why is it important to forgive people?

"15 A gentle answer turns away wrath,
but a harsh word stirs up anger."
Proverbs 15:1

Do you think Jesus calls us to be kind to only those who are like us? Those who agree with everything we do and like the things that we do?

What should you do if someone comes up to you and mocks you because you go to church? What if you don't know how to ride a bike yet, and they do, and they laugh at you?

Should you say something mean to them in return?
No.

The Bible says that a gentle answer turns away wrath, so that means when somebody is unkind to you, the best way to react is to put a smile on your face and just walk away.

That sounds a little hard, doesn't it?
It does, but we can do anything through Christ who gives us strength.

We need to wake up every single day and pray that Jesus would help us to be kind and love others. This includes those who seem unlovable. We cannot do it by ourselves. We can only do it with the help of God.

Do you trust Him?
He loves you, and he wants nothing more than to help you in times of need.
What would we do without Him?

~Time To Pray~

Lord, I am so thankful that I have You! Without You, life would be so much more difficult. Please continue to help me as I learn to love others as You love them. Help me to be kind even when it isn't easy. I pray that You'd help me to be just like You!
Amen!

KINDNESS CONVERSATIONS

Can you be kind without God's help?

What should you do when **you need God's help** with being more kind?

Does **God** ever get tired of **helping you?**

What is something you recently did for someone to **make them feel loved?**

"[3]Let love and faithfulness never leave you;
bind them around your neck,
write them on the tablet of your heart.
[4]Then you will win favor and a good name
in the sight of God and man."
Proverbs 3:3-4

There is nothing wrong with wanting to be liked by people. We all want to be loved and recognized for the great things we do!

Do you think that you should have to do whatever people want you to do, even if it's something wrong?
Something we know God would not want us to do?
Is being liked so important that you would steal or lie if someone asked you to?
Would you do this just because you wanted them to like you?
No way!

Nothing is worth going against God's word, causing you to make bad choices!

When we are kind and make the right kind of choices, we will attract good friends. Friends that help us make good choices and encourage us to draw closer to Jesus.

If someone doesn't bring out the best in us and doesn't bring out the GOD in us, then we need to choose to walk away and commit to praying for them.

Choosing honesty and kindness over popularity will always lead to God's approval and the approval of the right kind of people, and that is all that matters!

So, let's be kind and loving and trust that God is taking care of us and that He will bring us the kind of friends that He desires for us!

~Time To Pray~

Lord, today I pray that You would show me the people that are in my life who will always help me to act like You. Help me always to be honest and kind even if it means that some people won't like me as much. I pray that You would show me who I am in You so that approval from everyone wouldn't be so important to me! Thank You for teaching me, Jesus!
Amen.

KINDNESS CONVERSATIONS

Who is **your most kind friend?**

Do you have to pray for some of your friends to **be kinder?**

What are some things that **a good friend** does?
What about a bad friend?

34
Don't Give Up

"[9] Let us not become weary in doing good, for at the proper time we will reap a harvest if we do not give up."
Galatians 6:9

We have learned so much about kindness, haven't we?
Great work!

We also learned that being kind isn't always easy, is it? Sometimes we mess up and make the wrong choices. Do you know why? It's because we were born sinners.

None of us are perfect, and Jesus knows that.

He offers us His Grace and forgiveness, and He helps us as we try again and again. The important thing is that we should never give up!

As we practice being kind, it will become easier, and we won't have to try quite as hard.

Jesus is the best example of kindness, so make sure that you are studying his words in the Bible and keeping those words deep in your heart!

When you're faced with a hard decision or tough situation, His words will help you make the right choice!

Jesus loves you and wants you to succeed and be the best that you can be! Always look up to Him, and he will never lead you astray.

If all else fails, JUST BE KIND!

~Time To Pray~

Lord, thank You for always being there for me! Even if I can't see You, I know you are still there watching out for me. I pray that Your Holy Spirit would be alive in me and that I would be able to hear and feel when He is speaking to me and teaching me. Help me to be kind, just like You! **Amen!**

KINDNESS CONVERSATIONS

Do you feel like **you've learned to be more kind?**

What is **the kindest thing** that you have ever done for someone?

On a separate piece of paper, write down **how you feel when you are kind to someone. (If you can't write, just say it!)**

Coming Soon!

Anchored
in
Self-Control
A Fruit of the Spirit
Devotional for Kids
JENNA MAYE THOMPSON

Lightning Source UK Ltd.
Milton Keynes UK
UKHW022139100820
368019UK00005B/54

9 781735 256405